CODE ACADEMY

Perfect Program!

By Kirsty Holmes

CRABTREE
PUBLISHING COMPANY
WWW.CRABTREEBOOKS.COM

CRABTREE
PUBLISHING COMPANY
WWW.CRABTREEBOOKS.COM

Author:
Kirsty Holmes

Editorial director:
Kathy Middleton

Editors:
Emilie Dufresne, Crystal Sikkens

Proofreader:
Melissa Boyce

Graphic design:
Danielle Rippengill

Prepress technician:
Margaret Amy Salter

Print coordinator:
Katherine Berti

All images are courtesy of Shutterstock.com, unless otherwise specified. With thanks to Getty Images, Thinkstock Photo and iStockphoto.

Front Cover: Incomible, Nomad_Soul, teinstud, espies, udovichenko, Paisit Teeraphatsakool, STILLFX.

Interior: Background – teinstud. Characters: Ashwin – espies. Bailey – kravik93. Frankie – Kamira. Jia – PR Image Factory. Professor Chip – Elnur. Simon – YuryImaging. Sophia – MillaF. Ro-Bud – Carsten Reisinger. 5 – Iasha. 6–7 – Andrush. 7 – Ramy Fathalla. 12 – ByEmo. 15 – Inspiring, finevector. 16 – Rose Carson. 17 – Andrush. 19&20 – Luis Molinero.

All facts, statistics, web addresses, and URLs in this book were verified as valid and accurate at time of writing. No responsibility for any changes to external websites or references can be accepted by either the author or publisher.

Some lines of code used in this book have been constructed for comedic purposes, and are not intended to represent working code.

Library and Archives Canada Cataloguing in Publication

Title: Perfect program! / Kirsty Holmes.
Names: Holmes, Kirsty, author.
Description: Series statement: Code Academy | Includes index.
Identifiers: Canadiana (print) 20190098716 |
   Canadiana (ebook) 20190098740 |
   ISBN 9780778763437 (softcover) |
   ISBN 9780778763376 (hardcover) |
   ISBN 9781427123411 (HTML)
Subjects: LCSH: Computer programming—Juvenile literature.
Classification: LCC QA76.6115 .H65 2019 | DDC j005.1—dc23

Library of Congress Cataloging-in-Publication Data

Names: Holmes, Kirsty, author.
Title: Perfect program! / Kirsty Holmes.
Description: New York, New York : Crabtree Publishing, [2019] | Series: Code academy | Audience: Ages 5-7. | Audience: Grades: K-3. | Includes index.
Identifiers: LCCN 2019014224 (print) | LCCN 2019017524 (ebook) |
   ISBN 9781427123411 (Electronic) |
   ISBN 9780778763376 (hardcover) |
   ISBN 9780778763437 (pbk.)
Subjects: LCSH: Computer programming--Juvenile literature.
Classification: LCC QA76.6115 (ebook) | LCC QA76.6115 .H654 2019 (print)
   | DDC 005.1--dc23
LC record available at https://lccn.loc.gov/2019014224

Crabtree Publishing Company

www.crabtreebooks.com   1–800–387–7650

Published by Crabtree Publishing Company in 2020
© 2019 BookLife Publishing Ltd.

Printed in the U.S.A./072019/CG20190501

Published in Canada
Crabtree Publishing
616 Welland Ave.
St. Catharines, Ontario
L2M 5V6

Published in the United States
Crabtree Publishing
PMB 59051
350 Fifth Avenue, 59th Floor
New York, New York 10118

CONTENTS

Hi, I'm Finn and this is Ava. Welcome to the world of coding! In this book you will learn the basics of computers and coding.

After reading this book, join us online at *Crabtree Plus* to learn about logic, memory, and programming! Just use the Digital Code on page 23 in this book.

Words in bold, like **this**, can be found in the glossary on page 24.

ATTENDANCE

Code Academy is a school especially for kids who love computers and robots. Time to take attendance! Meet Class 101.

Sophia

Ashwin

Bailey

Simon

Jia

Frankie

Another day at Code Academy has begun. Today's lesson is all about **programming**. Programming means putting instructions into a computer. The class will find out the answers to these questions:

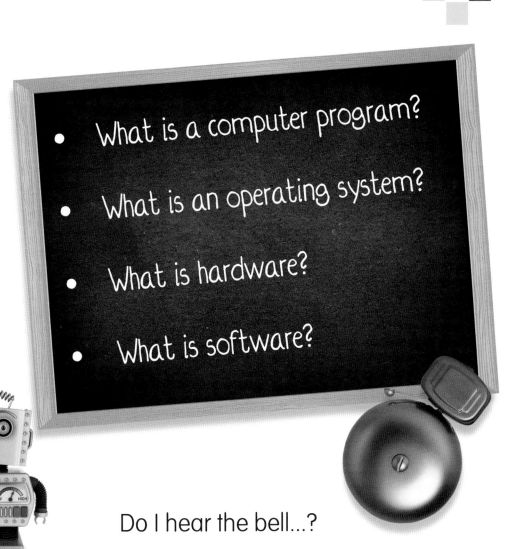

- What is a computer program?

- What is an operating system?

- What is hardware?

- What is software?

Do I hear the bell...?

Ro-Bud

The students' robot classmate

MORNING LESSON

Today, the students at Code Academy are working on their project—a **smart** car called CAT. CAT stands for computerized automatic transportation. That is another way of saying "a car that drives itself"!

OK, I think CAT is ready. Time to start her up!

First, the car will need to **charge** for a while.

CAT, how long will it take you to finish charging?

CAT TAKES ONE HOUR TO CHARGE COMPLETELY.

Perfect! She will be ready to drive after lunch.

LUNCHTIME!

The class goes to eat lunch while CAT charges.
But Ro-Bud notices that CAT is not plugged in.
She plugs in the power cord and...

ZZZAP!!

Oh no! Ro-Bud got an **electric shock**! It was not a big one, but it made her feel very strange.

Sophia Says:

Have you ever got a shock from touching something? Some objects, such as computers, can build up electricity on their surface. The shock you feel is the electricity flowing from that object to you. Always be very careful around electrical items!

GETTING HELP

The class comes back from lunch to find Ro-Bud looking very confused. She cannot seem to remember how to do anything.

RO-BUD REPORT?

RO-BUD RESTART?

RO-BUD WALK?

RO-BUD TALK?

LOW HIGH

Oh no! It looks like Ro-Bud got shocked. An electric shock can wipe out all the programs on a computer's **hard drive**.

Ro-Bud must have lost all the programs that tell her what to do. That's why she cannot remember how to move or talk.

TO THE WHITEBOARD!

Professor Chip takes the class to the whiteboard to discuss the problem.

We will need to **install** Ro-Bud's programs again to make her better. Let's list what programs she needs on the whiteboard.

PROGRAMS + OPERATING SYSTEMS

Computers can only do exactly what people tell them to. An instruction must be written for each thing a person wants the computer to do. The instructions are given to the computer through programs called software.

ASHWIN EXPLAINS

Computers use a lot of different programs to do different things. For example, you need to have a program called a web browser to see things on the Internet. To look at photographs, you need to have a program that can see pictures.

THE BIG BOOK OF PROGRAMS

The parts of a computer that you can see and touch are called hardware. Examples of hardware are the mouse, keyboard, and screen. Ro-Bud is hardware too!

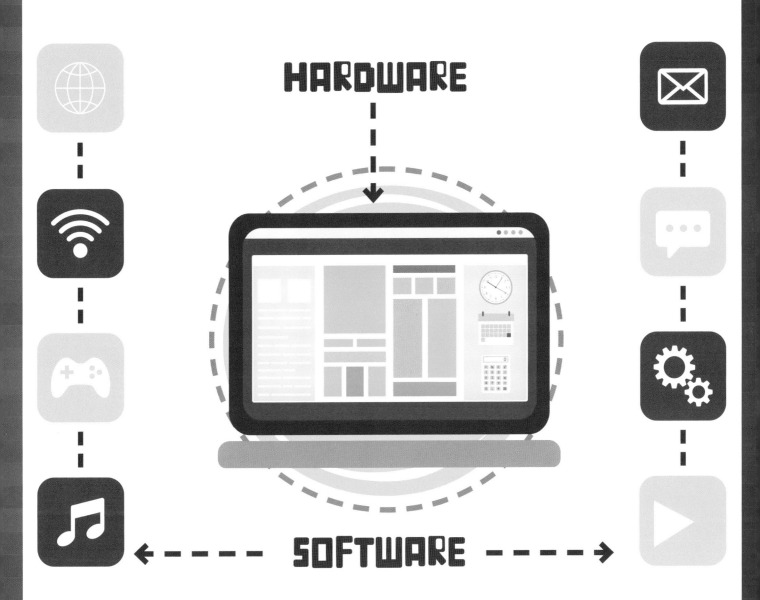

HARDWARE

SOFTWARE

The parts of a computer that you cannot see or touch are called software. You need software to make the hardware work.

The most important software program on a computer is the operating system, or OS for short. The OS software **translates** all the other software on the computer into instructions the hardware can understand.

Some popular examples of OS are Microsoft Windows, macOS, and Linux.

LET'S SEE HOW IT WORKS!

We added a program to CAT's OS. The program has instructions that tell CAT to drive to school.

PROGRAM
Contains instructions

OPERATING SYSTEM
Translates instructions

INSTRUCTIONS
Start engine
Find directions on map
Drive to school
Park at school parking lot
Shut off engine

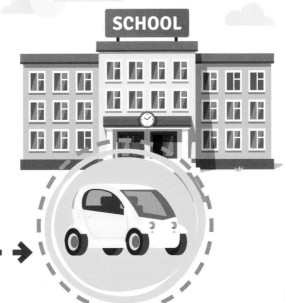

CAT has arrived at school!

A PERFECT PROGRAM

We know the shock wiped out Ro-Bud's programs. This means she doesn't know how to carry out any of her usual **functions**.

To help her, we need to install a new operating system and all her other programs. It is important to install the right program for the job.

Ashwin **downloads** Ro-Bud's operating system from the school server. Her OS is called CARS—the Code Academy Robotic System.

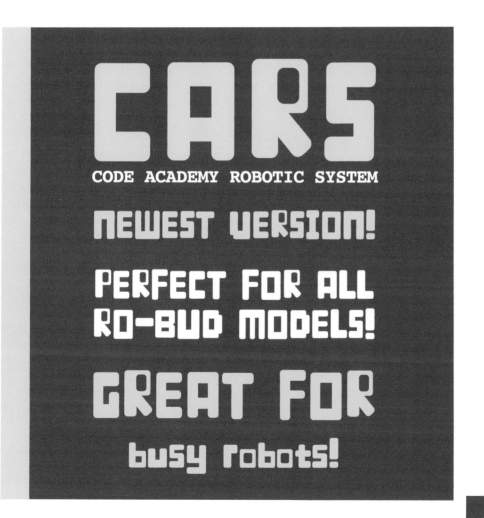

CARS
CODE ACADEMY ROBOTIC SYSTEM

NEWEST VERSION!

PERFECT FOR ALL RO-BUD MODELS!

GREAT FOR busy robots!

Ashwin is going to install Ro-Bud's new operating system now. Then we can install the rest of her software programs.

CARS

CODE ACADEMY ROBOTIC SYSTEM

NEWEST VERSION!

PERFECT FOR ALL RO-BUD MODELS!

GREAT FOR busy robots!

Install the OS on Ro-Bud's computer.

Choose the right OS for Ro-Bud's computer.

0100

0101

01000

101001

SINGING
READING
TALKING
DRAWING
PLAYING
SMILING

Ro-Bud should be working again!

Install all the other software she needs.

#1 ROBOT

21

SORTED OUT

Ro-Bud's new software works! She is soon back to herself again. Ashwin also added a program that will tell Ro-Bud how to be more careful when she plugs in electrical items.

HOMEWORK

Can you find all the programming words in this word search? Ask an adult to photocopy this page for you. Circle all the programming words from the list you can find.

H	A	R	D	W	A	R	E	T	M
U	W	T	F	Q	V	Y	H	K	I
S	K	P	F	C	S	N	D	G	N
W	J	W	C	P	C	R	E	A	T
U	P	R	O	G	R	A	M	T	E
C	T	B	D	T	E	M	O	E	R
I	E	G	E	W	E	Y	U	E	N
W	S	Y	L	K	N	J	S	A	E
S	O	F	T	W	A	R	E	M	T
P	V	B	M	E	S	T	I	N	L

HARDWARE
PROGRAM
SOFTWARE
SCREEN
MOUSE
INTERNET
CODE

For more fun activities, enter the code at the Crabtree Plus website below.

www.crabtreeplus.com/codeacademy

LOOK IT UP

GLOSSARY:

charge	To fill up with electrical power
download	To transfer files or software from one computer to the memory of another computer
electric shock	A sudden burst of electricity into the body
functions	The things a computer is instructed to do
hard drive	A device for storing memory
install	To put something into position, ready to use
programming	Putting instructions into a computer
smart	Technology that connects to the Internet
translate	To change the words of one language into another

INDEX: